Foreword

David Hallchurch has spent many yea a circuiteer practising in the Midlands before assuming judicial office, ending his judicial career as Chief Justice of the Turks and Caicos Islands.

During his professional life David witnessed or heard at immediate first hand of some of the moments of amusement and humour (usually unconscious) which occasionally punctuate the solemnity of the legal process. In this charming book he has recorded them and illustrated each story with his own delicately drawn sketches, skill no doubt developed as he doodled his way through the occasional interminable summing up, or long-winded judgement.

In "The Law is not a bore!", David pokes gentle fun at himself, both as a young officer doing his National Service, and as a Chief Justice, whose sentencing remarks were to be circulated to the local media to ensure that what he said could be readily understood. He also notices some of the foibles of his friends and colleagues, without for one moment causing offence or umbrage. All this is entirely in character. Those who know David recognise that although he is a clear sighted observer of the world and its foibles, he has always been and remains a civilised courteous man who would not deliberately cause offence or pain.

This little book will evoke a smile. It is for dipping into and browsing. It may well find its way into a Christmas stocking, assuming, that is, that anyone connected with the law has the nerve to believe it worthwhile to hang up a stocking in the hope that Father Christmas will deign to notice his or her good works for the year.

The Rt Hon Lord Igor Judge
Lord Chief Justice of England and Wales

THE LAW IS NOT A BORE

by

David Hallchurch

Published by David Hallchurch 2008

Copyright © David Hallchurch 2008

David Hallchurch has asserted his right under the Copyright, Designs and Patents Act 1988 to be identified as the author of this work. This book is sold subject to the condition that it shall not, by way of trade or otherwise, be lent, resold or hired out, or otherwise circulated without the publisher's prior consent in any form of binding or cover other than that in which it is published and without a similar condition, including this condition being imposed on the subsequent purchaser.

This book is dedicated to another man's wife, Joanna White, who inspired me; also to my own beloved wife Susan for her constant criticism!

CONTENTS

1. Introduction
2. A Close Run Thing
3. A Gleaming Error
4. Women Always Have The Last Word
5. Pupillage
6. A Woolly Exchange
7. A Naughty Wedding
8. Its Not Just Juries that are Well Hung
9. Documents Exchanged between Solicitors
9. One Question Too Many
11. A Real Blow
12. A Nullity Case
13. Young Love
14. A Bold Mitigator
15. Cell Graffiti
16. Poetic Licence At The Old Bailey
17. A Murder Trial in Botswana
18. Perils of a Visit to a Safari Park
19. The Court of Appeal
20. The House of Lords
21. The Turks and Caicos Islands
22. A Senior Solicitor's Day In Court
23. Miscellany:
(a) The Legendary Rigby Swift. J
(b) Overseas Judges
(c) A Victorian Poison Murder Case
(d) A Barrister's Attempt to be Humorous
(e) Three Snippets:
   As God be my Witness,
   A Judge's Plea,
   A Juror's Plea.

1. INTRODUCTION

A barristers robing room is the focal point for humour. Barristers arrive between that all important hour of 9.15am to 10.15am, prepared and ready to do battle and sometimes to negotiate. In either case they need to appear confident and the atmosphere is tense, but invariably someone cracks a joke and the tension eases. Later, when they return to their respective chambers and relax, further jokes and stories will be recounted.

The true stories in this edition of 'The Law is not a Bore' come from my recollection over forty years in practice both here and overseas. I have also added a few old chestnuts from years gone by. My colleagues have their own stories to tell and no doubt those practising today are feeding on humorous anecdotes as we did.

The stories of today's practitioners will be as good or even better than my own recollections. The only advantage I have is that after years of doodling I recapture the scenario to some extent in my sketches.

If you are intelligent and have an imagination you should enjoy these reminiscences. Read on.

2. A CLOSE RUN THING

In the early 1950's two years National Service was obligatory. I chose the army, and after receiving a commission was posted to a regiment stationed at Barnard Castle, Co Durham. It was a cold mid-winter day when I became orderly officer; entrusted to go on tour at night, call out the guard, inspect various places and as the Sergeant's mess were holding a party, to pop in and have a drink with them as they liked to see their young officers socially from time to time, or so I was told. Anyway, as a
dutiful young officer I did as I was bid and finished up in the Sergeant's mess at about 1am. I took off my snow covered great coat and sat with a group of Sergeants and their wives. After a while, I invited one wife to dance and was accepted. As soon as we reached the dance floor the lights were dimmed and a slow dance tune was played. My partner closed in on me and I responded dutifully, but without enthusiasm. After a short while, my blond companion looked up at me and cooed, "Are yo in luv with me?" "No" I spluttered and led her back to our table. I thanked her for the dance and she giggled and whispered into her husband's ear.
I beat a hasty retreat, put on my great coat, searched for my torch and found it in my left trouser pocket!
I broke out in a cold sweat as a court martial loomed up in my vivid imagination!

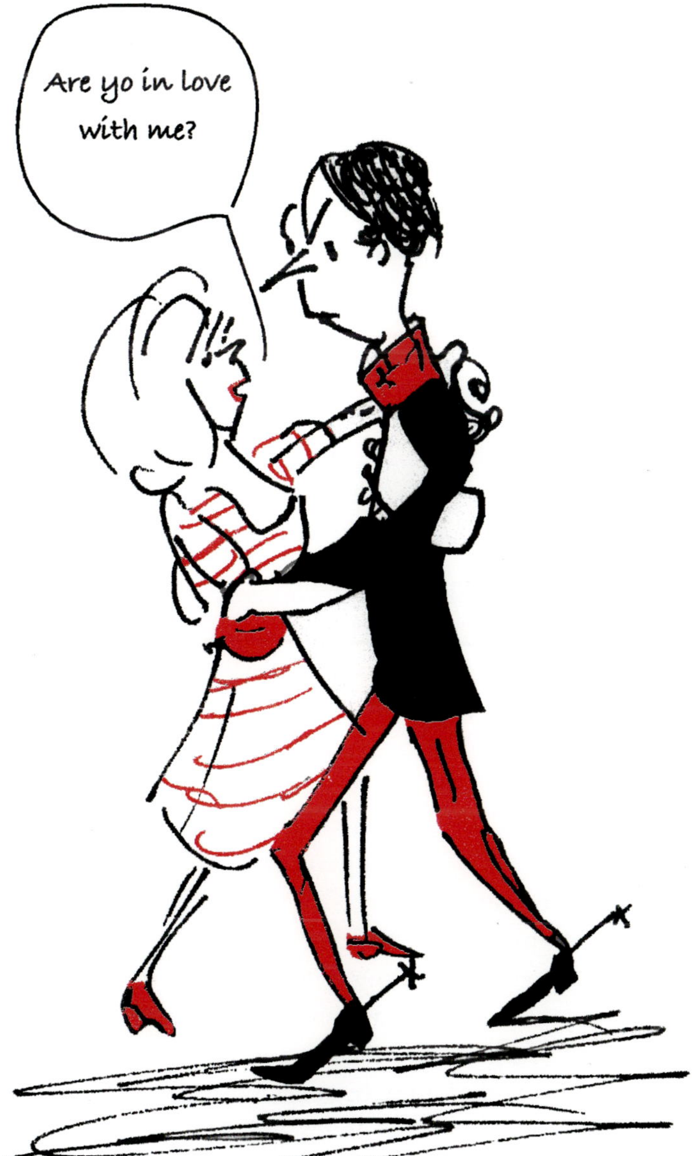
Are yo in love
with me?

3 A GLEAMING ERROR

"Out of touch with popular culture" is still a common accusation levelled at judges across Britain, especially by the tabloid media.

"Who's this Paul Gascoigne?" one asked around the time the footballer had been sent off in a European Championship semi-final and his tears were splashed across the sports pages.

Judges are now far more in touch than they ever used to be, but I've seen plenty who seemed to be more in tune with good claret and a night at the opera than the antics of David Beckham or the Big Brother house.

One of my earliest recollections goes back to 1950 when I was a law student at Oxford and deciding whether to become a barrister.

The scene was Shrewsbury Assizes, where a High Court Judge's visit to a rural market town was something of an occasion. His lofty magnificence was exaggerated by all the pomp and ceremony that preceded the sitting at the senior criminal court. First there was a church service. Then the judge was driven to the court in a cavalcade, accompanied by the sound of the trumpets, drums and the marching feet of a military band. Quite an occasion for the folk of this quaint Shropshire town.

Finally, the scarlet robed and bewigged judge took his place in his high seat, from where he could survey his court.

The clerk, clearly humbled by the presence of a High Court Judge, read out the writs and there was much deferential bowing and scraping before the work finally started.

First on were three young army recruits who stood nervously in the dock, accused of theft. They pleaded guilty. A tall pompous barrister then outlined the case. The three lads had broken into the shop at their barracks – known as the NAAFI – after a night out on the town. They had ignored the cash register, and anything else that might have been worth a few bob. Instead, their attention was drawn to half a dozen bottles of Brylcream. At the time the hair treatment was an essential commodity for any young man about town. No doubt, they had been seduced by the many adverts featuring the legendary batsman, Dennis Compton – the Kevin Pieterson of his day. His gleaming, slicked-back hair was impossible to miss in magazines, newspapers and on poster billboards across the country. It was well known that Compton, who also played football for Arsenal, had won the adoration of thousands of young women – a fact which no doubt spurred on our three young soldiers.

Suddenly, the pompous prosecutor was rudely interrupted by the judge, who roared: "What is Brylcream?"

The prosecutor was taken aback by surprise and spluttered some kind of definition before moving on quickly to distract the packed court away from the judge's ignorance.

The old judge, seemingly impervious to embarrassment, finally decided that he shouldn't have been trying the case anyway and ruled that the case should be heard before a Court Martial. Fortunately, the local newspaper reporter was not as vigilant or as unforgiving as today's hacks, and the judge wasn't publicly vilified in the same way he might have been today for such a remark.

That's about as interesting as it got in the Shrewsbury court which suffered from a lack of serious cases and now has no visiting High Court Judge.

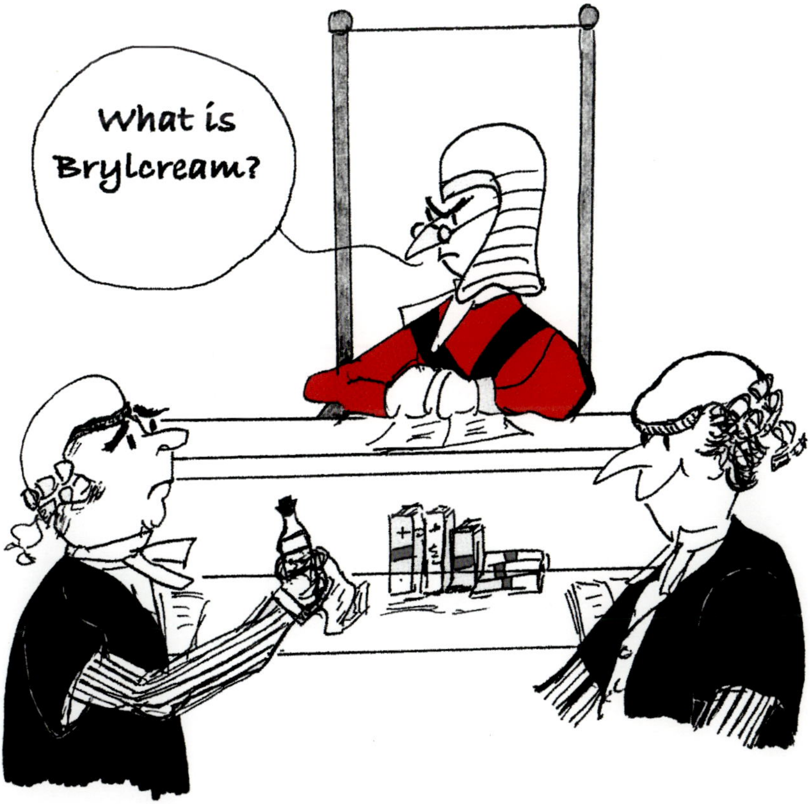
What is Brylcream?

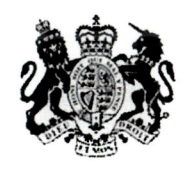

4. WOMEN ALWAYS HAVE THE LAST WORD

You always remember a good teacher. One who sticks in my mind is Robert Megarry QC, who later became a High Court Judge. At the time he was speaking on a course of legal education lectures in London and his brilliance succeeded in livening up a series of talks on equity, which I've always found very dull.

One of his cases was about a henpecked husband who made a will leaving all his worldly goods to the local parish church on condition that the church bells were rung on the anniversary of his death celebrating his release from his *unhappy marriage*!

When he eventually died and his will was read his widow was shocked and humiliated. But she was a practical woman and not one to be beaten by anything or anyone let alone her dead husband. She found an able lawyer and challenged the validity of the will. He was articulate and persuasive, aided by his client's mournful presence. The Court held that the bell ringing was contrary to public policy and the will was declared null and void. So once again, *she had the last word*!

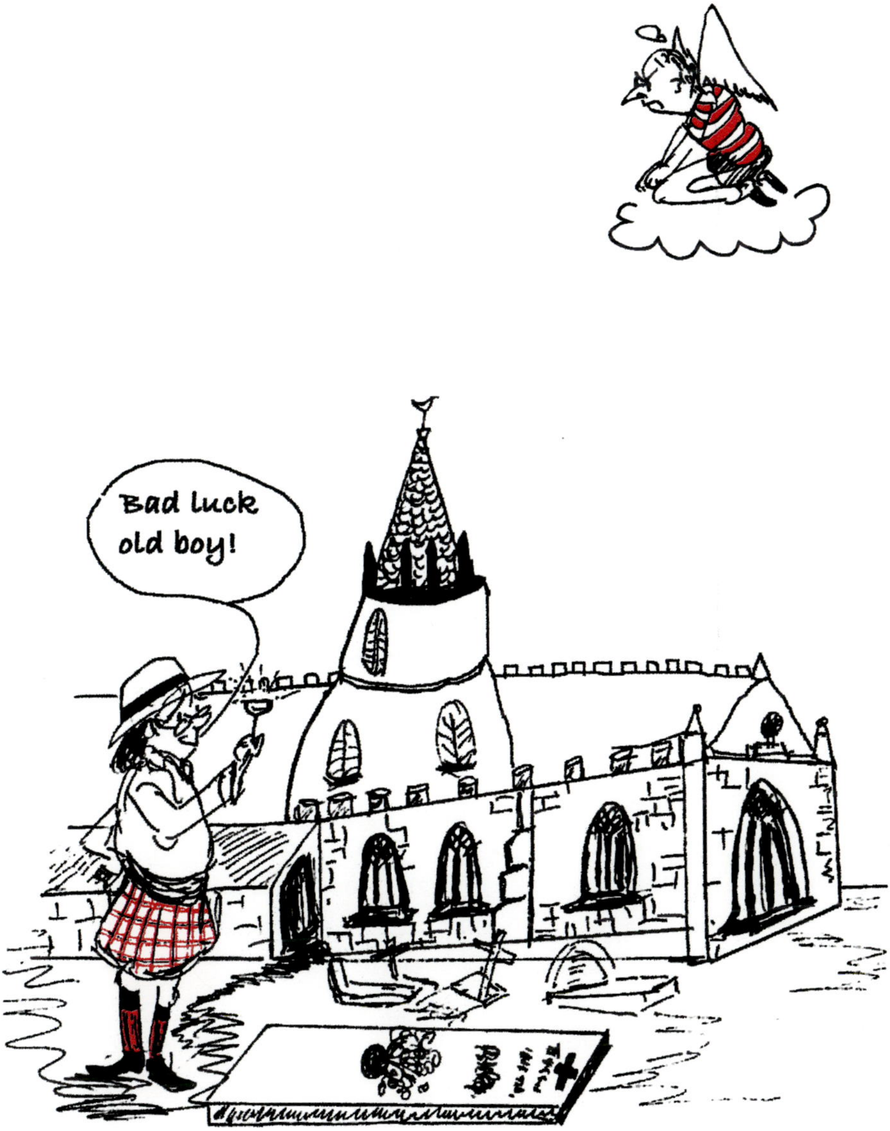
Bad luck old boy!

5. PUPILLAGE

I was called to the Bar by Gray's Inn in 1953 and gained a pupillage in chambers in Birmingham. For six months I was pupil to the Head of Chambers, a senior barrister who spent most of his time in London. In his absence, I accompanied other senior barristers to various courts on the Oxford circuit (now the Midland circuit). One of these barristers took me to an Assize where I discovered that being hard of hearing was no detriment to the bench. There was no retiring age for High Court judges in those days.

If a defendant pleaded guilty or was convicted by a jury, his counsel addressed the court in mitigation. When he had finished it was practice in those days for the clerk of Assize to ask the defendant if he had anything to say before sentence was passed. On this occasion, the clerk duly asked the question to which the defendant replied: "Bugger all".
The judge did not hear what the defendant had said and tapped the top of his desk with his pen. The clerk of Assize turned to face him, and the judge asked:
"What did he say?"
"Bugger all M'lord" replied the clerk, whereupon the judge said:
"Uhm, I'm sure I saw his lips move"!

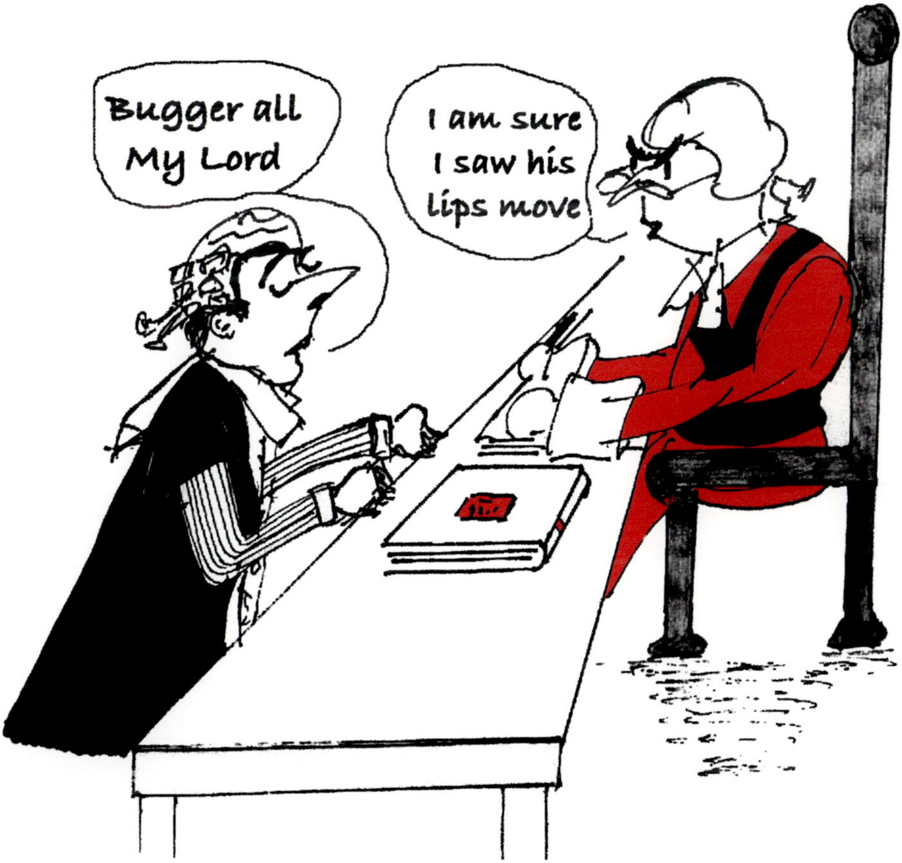
Bugger all My Lord
I am sure I saw his lips move

6. A WOOLLY EXCHANGE

During my pupillage I went with a senior barrister to another Assize, and I listened to the trial of a man charged with committing an unsavoury act with a sheep, more common than you might expect in rural areas in those days. I watched in raptures as the clerk and judge became entangled in the strange rules of English pronunciation.

Clerk to the accused: "You are charged with committing an act of outraging public decency in that you on the 5th day of November 1954 committed an act of a lewd, obscene and disgusting nature, outraging public decency by behaving in an indecent manner with a ewe (pronounced 'eewee' by the clerk) to the great disgust and annoyance of divers of her Majesty's subjects within whose purview such act was committed."

Judge to clerk: "Put it again."

Clerk to the accused: "You are charged with committing an act of outraging public decency in that you on the 5th day of November 1954 committed an act of a lewd, obscene and disgusting nature, outraging public decency by behaving in an indecent manner with an eewee.."

Judge to clerk: "Stop! 'Ewe', 'Ewe'," he shouted, no longer able to tolerate the clerk's clumsy mispronunciation.

Clerk to Judge: "No, no, not me m'lord," he said sheepishly.

7. A NAUGHTY WEDDING

Barristers have a poor public profile. People know that courts don't sit from 9am to 5.30pm which are the hours most people work, so they assume that barristers have an easy life. What most never see, so never really think about, are the long hours barristers spend working on papers writing opinions, drafting pleadings and settling indictments, often at home alone when most people are watching television.

These duties are crucial to the judicial process, and it's important that barristers pay meticulous attention to detail. The court is a very public arena, and there is no hiding from mistakes. Early in my career this became very clear to me during a divorce hearing.

In those days (1950's) a petitioner had to disclose adultery by filing a statement for the judge which concluded with the prayer:
'The petitioner humbly prays that this honourable court will grant him/her a decree nisi of divorce notwithstanding his/her adultery committed since the celebration of the marriage'.

I must have been tired and a little careless when I was working on the petition – or maybe I was enjoying the afterglow of a good dinner – because I managed to insert the work 'during' instead of 'since', which changed the meaning of the poor petitioner's application quite radically.

I did discover my error the night before I went to court but by then the judge had his own copy of the petition. I just prayed that the old County Court Judge would not notice my error but he did and with a twinkle in his eye and a broad smile to me, he said:
"Yes, I grant a decree nisi of divorce notwithstanding the petitioner's adultery committed during the celebration of the marriage."

I went several shades of crimson, but it was a good lesson about the need to pay fastidious attention to detail – and one I never forgot.

8. IT'S NOT JUST JURIES THAT ARE WELL –HUNG.

A young barrister was a 'jack of all trades' in provincial chambers such as Birmingham in the 1950s. You accepted a brief involving anything including copyright, defamation and Landlord and Tenant cases. There were no specialists except those practising in Chancery and Town and Country Planning matters. However, for the most part you 'cut your teeth' on dangerous or careless driving cases in the Magistrates' Court.

I remember receiving a brief to defend a sad young man who had been accused of dressing up in his raincoat, boots and not much else before going into a well-known department store and flashing to a young woman shop assistant. I was very amused by her witness statement, in which she testified that the defendant had exposed himself in front of her, but added:
"You could have hung eight coat hangers on it."
I wondered if the police investigating the crime had considered an identity parade.

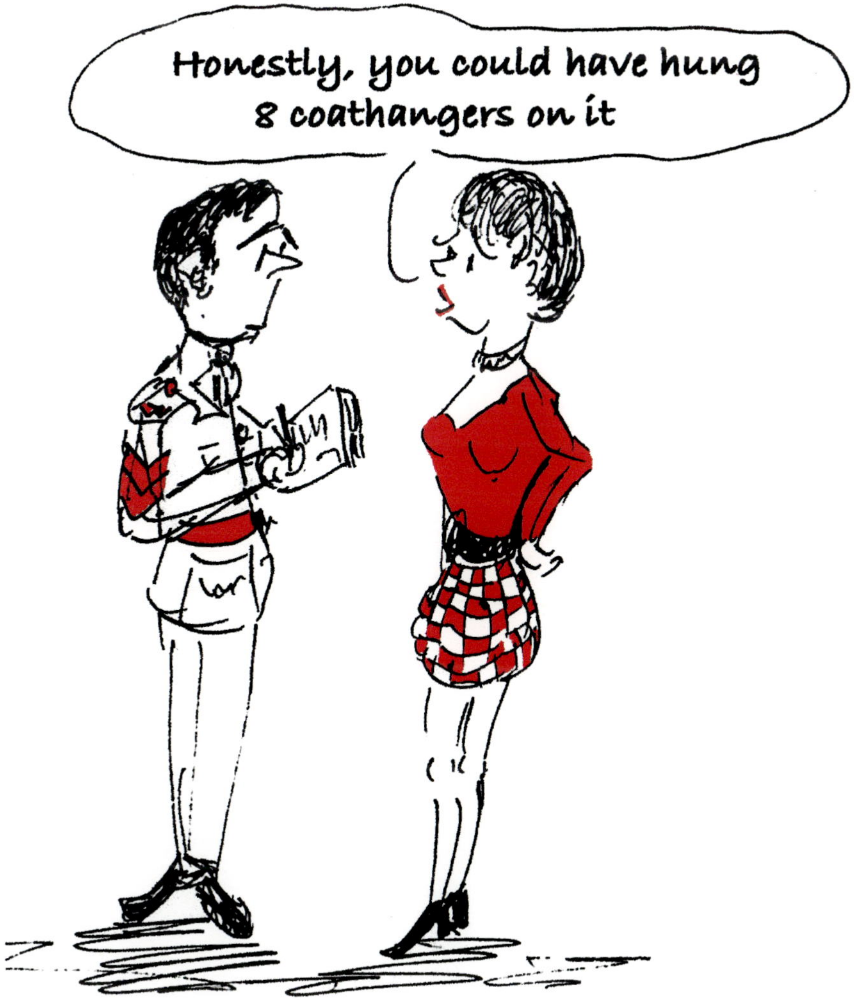
Honestly, you could have hung 8 coathangers on it

9. DOCUMENTS EXCHANGED BETWEEN SOLICITORS

Whilst working in chambers one afternoon, one of my colleagues interrupted us. He was reading his brief in a long divorce case where each side was alleging adultery based on the fact that each had been infected with venereal disease.

During the long and protracted correspondence between solicitors one of them, rather sensibly, suggested that they should exchange medical reports to see who had contracted V.D. first in time. The other solicitor agreed and in due course medical reports were exchanged.

It transpired that one had contracted gonorrhoea and the other syphilis!

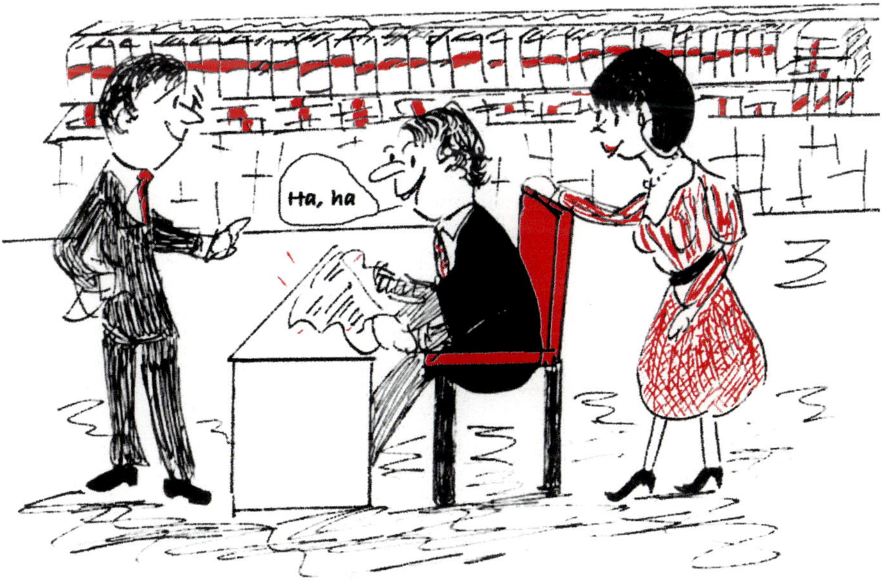
Ha, ha

10. ONE QUESTION TOO MANY

At Warwick Quarter Session, three defendants were being tried for a joint shop breaking offence committed in the early hours of the morning in the middle of Warwick. Each defendant ran an alibi defence, i.e. he was somewhere else when the crime was committed.

The prosecution's main claim was one of identification. A police officer giving evidence said he had seen and identified one defendant standing on the corner of a street at about 3 o'clock in the morning. His defending barrister rose to cross examine and the crucial question and answer exchange went as follows:

Counsel: "Are you seriously suggesting that you travelled from the top of the street to within a few yards of my client before he ran off?"
Police Officer: "Yes, sir."
Counsel: "The street is cobbled is it not?"
Police Officer: "Yes, sir."
Counsel: "Were you wearing policemen's boots with hobnails?"
Police Officer: "Yes, sir."
Counsel: "Those hobnails would grind into the cobblestones would they not, and make an appreciable noise?"
Police Officer: "Yes, sir."

Counsel: "How come, officer, that my client never heard you travelling some thirty yards to the corner of the street before he ran off?"
Police Officer: "Because I was on my bicycle, sir."

11. A REAL BLOW

Sometimes you end up with a client who, you feel, would have committed far worse crimes if only he'd been a bit smarter. Young Bert, a factory worker from West Bromwich, was one such lad. He was tough, lean and loyal like they make them in the Black Country, and followed the Baggies with unwavering loyalty, but wasn't the sharpest tool in the box.

He enjoyed his job at the West Bromwich meat-packing factory, but he was his own man and didn't like taking orders from anyone. He was used to a scrape or two with authority, but won respect for his hard work, and rarely missed a day. So it came as a shock when his foreman called him into his office and dismissed him for insubordination. It didn't help that the foreman wasn't exactly polite about him, and he felt humiliated when he had to tell the other lads.

He was so incensed that he brooded for days. Eventually he parked his old banger of a car in a car park next to the factory, where he had a clear view of the gates. He waited until the foreman finished work and appeared at the factory gates on his motorbike. He noted the time. Every day it was a quarter past five, and not a moment sooner or later. Then he followed cautiously behind him, as the bike trundled through the streets of terraced houses. Bert noted that the journey always took about 15 minutes. His former boss would park the motorbike in a shed next to his detached house. Bert also noted that the house was quite a lot larger than the terraced house where he was still living with his mum.

Slowly, Bert worked out how he would even the scores and really teach his boss a lesson.

On the fourth day, he made sure that he was at the foreman's home at five o'clock. He hid himself among the cartons and boxes in the shed. As expected, the foreman arrived home at 5.30pm and started wheeling his bike into the shed. He had quite a shock when young Bert leapt from behind a tea chest, aiming a hammer blow at his head. But it was a greater shock to Bert when the hammer bounced harmlessly from his foreman's crash helmet, something he'd failed to notice during his hours of observation. I couldn't help thinking that if he'd been a bit brighter he'd have been facing a murder charge.

12. A NULLITY CASE

In the 1950s there were numerous divorces following quick and impulsive marriages during World War II. The lawyers, especially the barristers, found the work easy and rewarding as most of the cases were undefended. In order to succeed as a practitioner you needed to prove your case succinctly so as to appease the judge who nearly always had a long list to get through.

On one occasion, Malcolm Lee, (later, a QC and the first Mercantile Judge in Birmingham) was dealing with a case of nullity. He was alleging that the marriage had not been consummated. His client was a Polish lady who had married a British soldier in Berlin and as she spoke little English a Polish national was called to act as interpreter.

The crucial questions and answers went as follows:

Counsel: "After your wedding did you spend the first night in a hotel in Berlin?"
Interpreter: "Yes."
Counsel: "Did anything happen?"
Interpreter: "No."
Counsel: "Did you spend the next three days in a hotel in Amsterdam on the way back to England?"
Interpreter: "Yes."

Counsel: "Did anything happen?"
Interpreter: "No."
Counsel: "After you returned to England, did you cohabit with your husband for five weeks before leaving him?"
Interpreter: "Yes."
Counsel: "Did anything happen?"
Interpreter: "No."

Malcolm Lee then turned to the judge and said: "On that evidence, M'lord, I pray for a decree nisi of nullity."

The judge hesitated for a moment and then said: "Mr Lee, I have to decide whether the non-consummation of the marriage was due to wilful refusal or incapacity."

"Quite so M'lord, I will put some further questions to my client."

Further questions and answers went like this:

Counsel: "Did your husband have an erection whilst you were staying in your hotel in Berlin?"
Interpreter: "No."
Counsel: "Did he ever have an erection during your honeymoon in Amsterdam?"
Interpreter: "No."
Counsel: "During your five weeks of cohabitation in England did he ever have an erection?"

There was a rather longer exchange between the interpreter and the Polish lady and eventually this answer was given:

Interpreter: "Yes, he had an apartment in Wimbledon!"

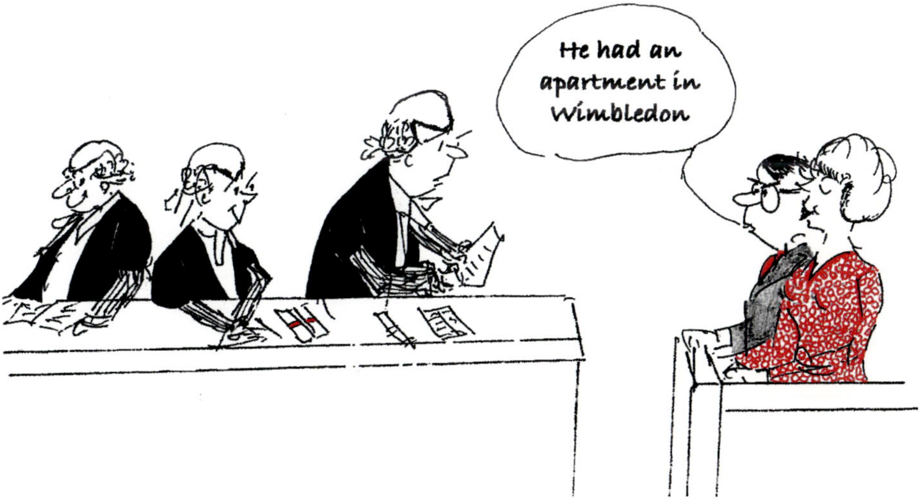
He had an apartment in Wimbledon

13. YOUNG LOVE

A young counsel appeared on behalf of a nineteen year old youth who had pleaded guilty to having unlawful sexual intercourse with a fifteen year old girl (sixteen is the age of consent). The exchange between judge and counsel went as follows:

Junior Counsel: "These two young people were overcome by their feelings, they were deeply in love."
Judge: "I see."
Junior Counsel: "The Defendant's behaviour was motivated by love, not lust. There is a vital distinction, as your Lordship knows."
Judge: (Not unkindly) "Yes, I think I know that. It is rather like the distinction between principle and prejudice. I have principles and you have prejudices."

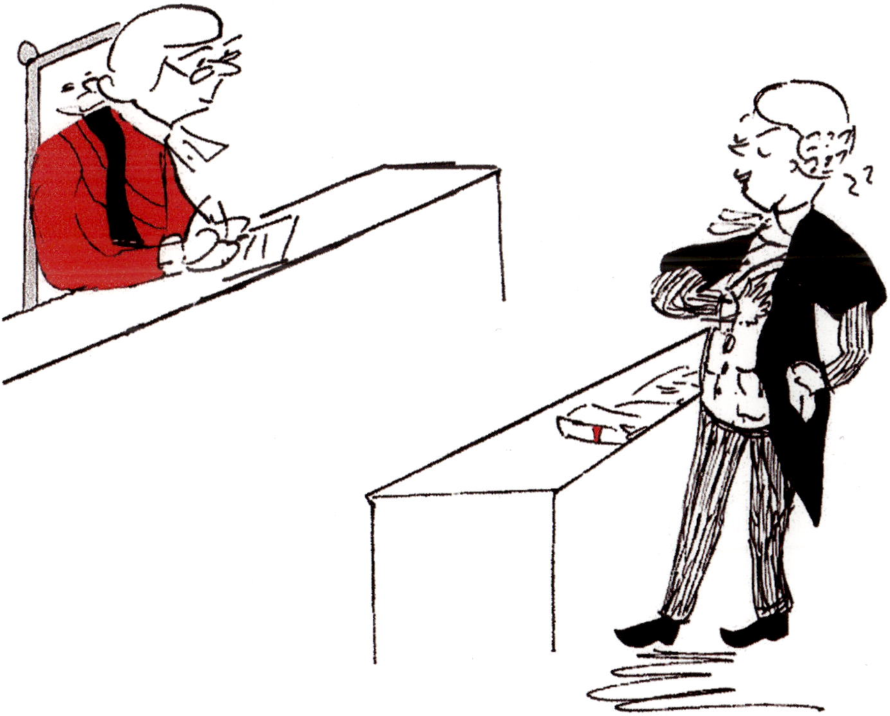

14. A BOLD MITIGATOR

Mr X was addressing Fred Lawson J, a highly experienced judge, in mitigation following his client's pleas of guilty to certain coinage offences. The crucial exchange between judge and counsel went as follows:

Judge: "This is a serious case, it calls for a substantial sentence."
Counsel: "I respectfully disagree with your Lordship."
Judge: "This class of offence is always dealt with by a long sentence Mr X."
Counsel: "I have to suggest that the Court of Appeal may take a different view."
Judge: "Mr X, may I remind you that I sit in the Court of Appeal."
Counsel: "Then your Lordship will know that I am right."

The spontaneous titters of laughter around the court soon faded away before the fixed icy smile of the judge. A few days later I met Mr X at the same Assizes and he confided in me that he had not pushed his luck before the same judge again.

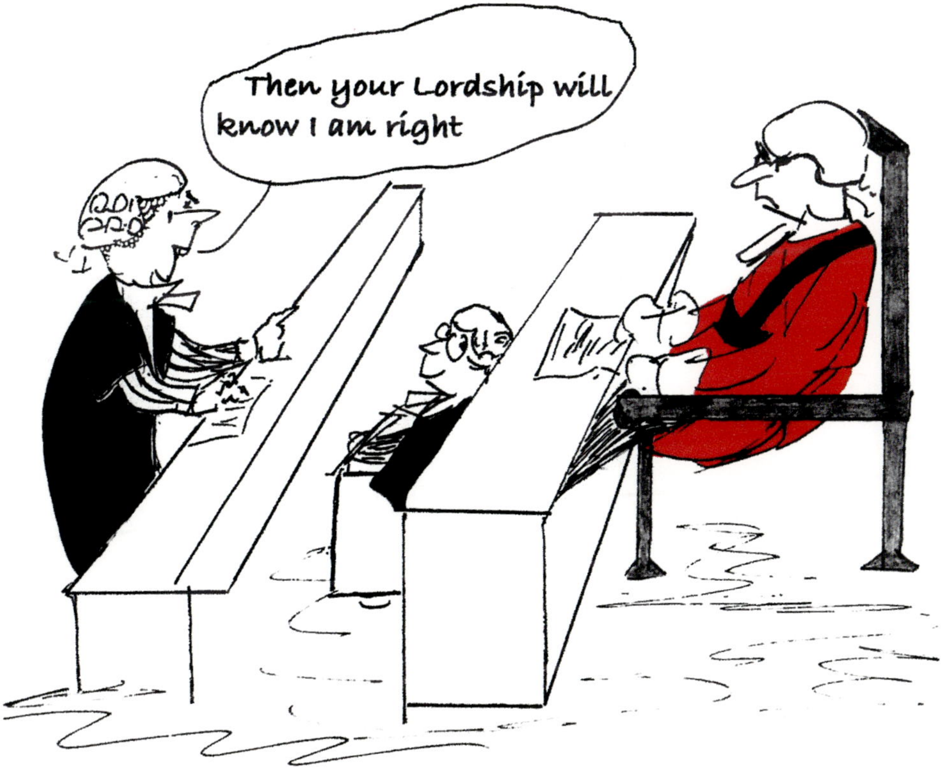
Then your Lordship will know I am right

15. CELL GRAFFITI

At Shrewsbury Crown Court, I arrived well in time to visit my client in his cell before the trial started. A female clerk accompanied me from my instructing solicitor's office. After introducing myself to the client, but before opening my brief, my eyes fell upon some graffiti on the wall behind my client's bed that read:
'My mum wanted me to be a judge but I was illegible (ineligible) because my dad married my mum.'

In other words he wasn't a bastard but all judges were. At least my client had a sense of humour!

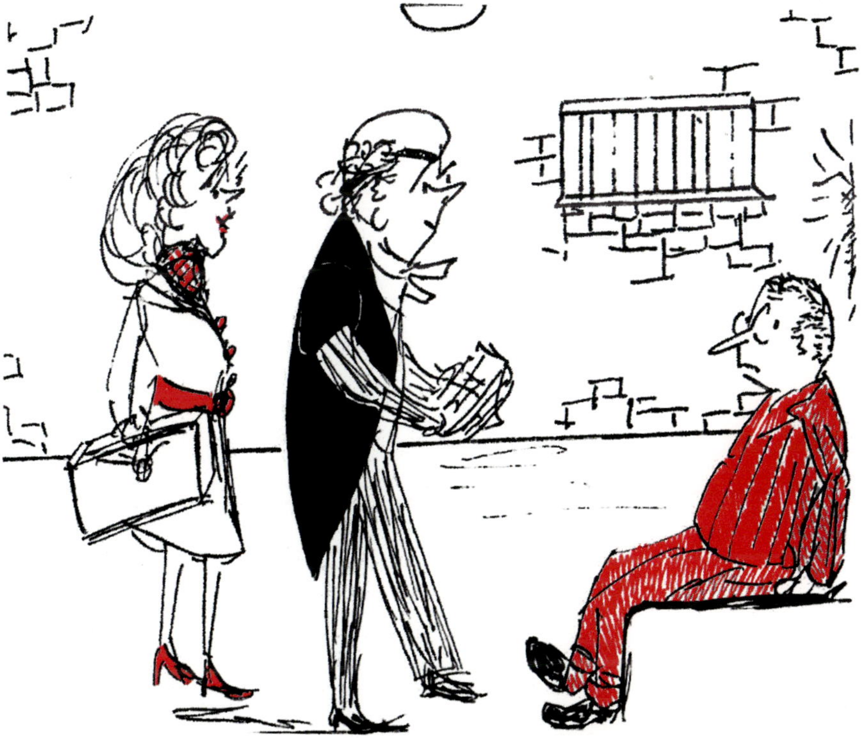

16. POETIC LICENCE AT THE OLD BAILEY

Every now and again, we Circuiteers would have to go to the 'smoke' (London) either to play on the Centre Court - Central Criminal Court, Old Bailey - or to face the judges in the Court of Appeal, or on occasions the judges in the House of Lords. On one of my visits to the Old Bailey, a sunny Friday, I had only one case (a plea) to deal with and I was anxious to return home as soon as possible. Having made an early start by train from Birmingham I went to the robing room at the Old Bailey at about 9.45a.m. I walked around the room that was beginning to fill up with barristers, who were strangers to me, and saw on the list that I was in Court 19 and was being prosecuted by one Mr Daniel Acram.
I ascertained that 'Tinker', as Acram was called, was in the room and introduced myself to him.
I then informed him of the case that we were in, and asked him if he would be prepared to accept a plea of guilty from my client to Section 20 (unlawful wounding) rather than the more serious charge of Section 18 (wounding with intent).

After a short pause, my colleague said:
"Yes, I don't see any problem with that. Section 20 is perfectly acceptable and the Judge won't be any problem either."

I was relieved to hear that and I then asked him how long he thought it might be before I could get away.

'Don't worry Old Sport, its POETS day today."

This he later explained meant:

'Piss off early tomorrow's Saturday!'

17. A MURDER TRIAL IN BOTSWANA

In Botswana, the penalty for murder was death by hanging unless there were extenuating circumstances when a term of imprisonment could be imposed. A trial took place before a judge alone and there was no jury and no assessors. It was entirely up to the judge to decide whether the accused was guilty or not and then to pass sentence.

In most of the murders I tried I was able to find extenuating circumstances, but there came into my list a case where a jealous husband was convinced that his wife was having an affair with a neighbour. One night, in the height of the summer season when his wife was asleep outside on her mat, he crept out of his rondavel armed with a pickaxe. He stood over her and split open her head with one fatal blow of the pickaxe. It was premeditated murder and the gallows loomed.

I was extremely concerned because in England, a psychiatrist would in all probability have been called to say that the accused was suffering from diminished responsibility at the time he committed the act and in all the circumstances the accused would probably have been convicted of manslaughter. The defence of diminished responsibility was not available in Botswana, so I was in a quandary. Also, there was very little legal aid available and as the defence counsel were very poorly paid the advocates did not always devote as much time as they should have in preparing their cases.

However, it so happened that in Lobatse where the High Court was situated, there was not only the biggest abattoir in the southern hemisphere but the one and only Mental hospital in Botswana. So I took the opportunity to visit the hospital and seek out its top psychiatrist who was an Indian. He was a pleasant affable man and he appreciated quite quickly the difficulty I was facing in this case, and without hesitation he undertook to see the accused in prison and to read all the depositions in the trial papers. He also agreed to come and sit in court during the trial and was quite prepared to give evidence at the end of the trial. I thanked him very much and left the documents with him. I felt I had done enough for the accused in this case.

Eventually the trial took place and in accordance with his word, there was the psychiatrist sitting quietly in court and listening to all that was said.

At an appropriate time I, off my own bat, called the psychiatrist into the witness box. He appeared confident and described his interviews with the defendant in prison.

I then asked him the $64,000 question:
"What do you think the defendant's state of mind was when he struck the pickaxe through his wife's head?"

To which the he replied:
"How should I know, I wasn't there!"

There was a pause, a lengthy pause, while I recovered from the shock of his reply. I had expected him to say that the man was so distraught by the thought of his wife's infidelity that he was acting abnormally, completely out of character, and that in effect he was suffering from diminished responsibility.

I had to find him guilty of murder on the evidence but I still managed to find that extenuating circumstances existed and thereby avoided having to impose the death penalty. He was sentenced to 15 years imprisonment which was upheld in the Court of Appeal.

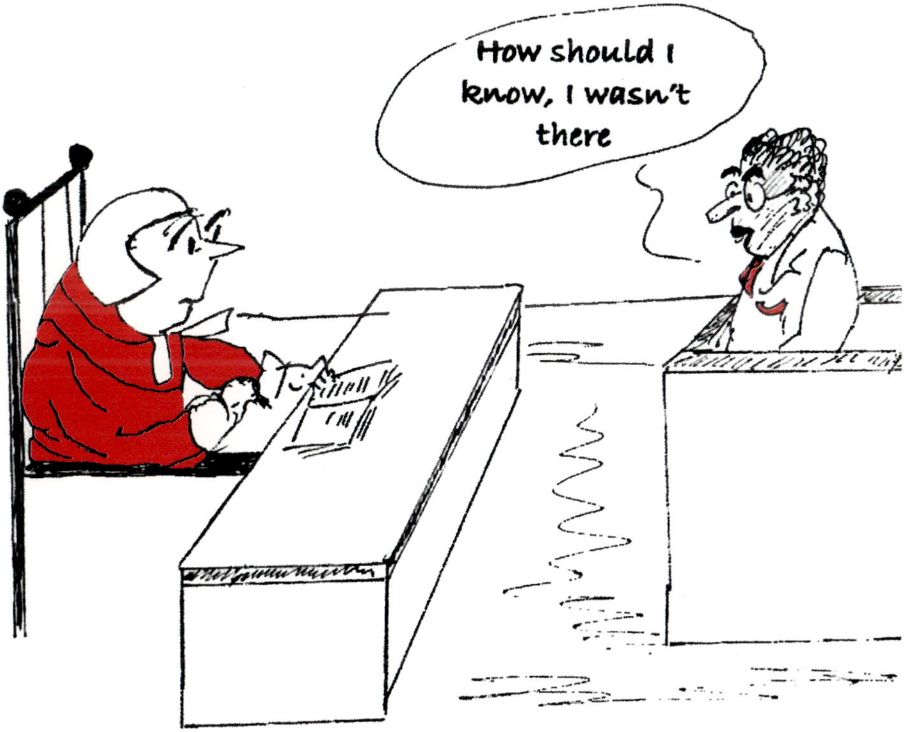
How should I know, I wasn't there

18. PERILS OF A VISIT TO A SAFARI PARK

I returned on leave from abroad and went to visit my old chambers in Fountain Court, Birmingham. Just as I was entering the building I met a friend coming out who had recently been appointed a QC. After exchanging a few pleasantries I asked him what he was doing and he said he was off to a Magistrate's Court. I raised my eyebrows and asked what he was doing appearing in a Magistrates' Court when he was now an exalted Queen's Counsel. He replied:

"Ah! My client is a very rich man and it's quite an unusual case," and he went on to tell me this story.

'My client was driving his family in his Silver Cloud Rolls Royce through a Safari Park on quite a chilly day. Eventually they stopped for lunch and due to the inclement weather they decided to have their picnic inside the car. While they were eating their lunch - my client actually had a pork pie in his hand - an elephant's trunk suddenly came through the driver's window and took hold of the pie. Shocked and taken completely by surprise he pressed the button on his electric window, which rose trapping the elephant's trunk. Suddenly, it was the elephant that was shocked and as he tried to extract his trunk from the driver's window he began to pound the side of the Rolls Royce until my client's wife bent over and pressed the window button releasing the elephant's trunk.

Still in shock and appearing to have had some sort of heart attack my client drove to the warden's lodge where he recounted what had happened. The wardens were extremely apologetic and from their medicine chest they produced some brandy which they offered to my client, who happily downed a few slugs. After a while, when he appeared completely recovered he shook hands with the wardens and set off back to Birmingham with his family.

They had only just got onto the motorway when they hit a long tail back as there had been a serious accident further up the motorway. While waiting in the queue a police car went by, but just after passing my client's Rolls Royce it stopped, reversed and two policemen got out and approached my client. One of them said to him as he sat in his car:
"Excuse me sir, can you explain how these dents were made in the side of your car?"
My client replied: "Well it was like this officer. I was in the Safari Park having my lunch when suddenly this elephant's trunk appeared through my window and took away my pork pie."
At this point the officer nodded and with a smile on his face said:
"Do you mind getting out and just blowing into this bag?"

Of course the result was positive and he was taken off to the police station and later charged with driving with excess alcohol. A most unfortunate end to a day in the Safari Park.'

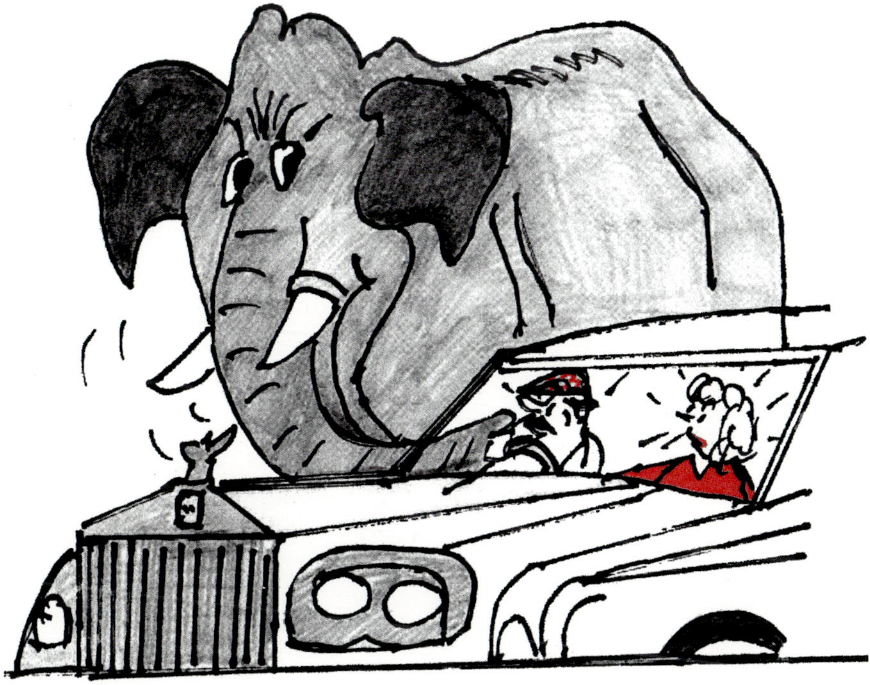

19. THE COURT OF APPEAL

Humour was for the judge, and tittering or smiling was obligatory for counsel. Only occasionally did counsel chance his luck, and he did so at his peril. However, the Court of Appeal was probably the best place to play your card, because if you got it right, at least two judges might be amused.

Appeals against sentence were fairly common and a long list of appeals were listed on the same day, usually before three judges sometimes two. On one occasion I was waiting patiently for my case to come on when I heard this exchange between Bench and Bar. One of her Majesty's Judges interrupted a barrister in full flow by snapping:
"Is this case going to last all week?"
The barrister concerned remained completely unflappable and calmly took a rail ticket out of his waistcoat pocket. Holding it up before their Lordships he said:
"A day return to Liverpool, m'lord."

Is this case going to last all week?
Day return to Liverpool M'Lud

20. THE HOUSE OF LORDS

A leading criminal silk (QC) told me of his first appearance in the House of Lords. He had a weak case and was given a rough ride by their Lordships, who sit in lounge suits whilst counsel is fully robed. Eventually their Lordships stopped asking questions and my friend was allowed to continue his submissions without interruption. His confidence began to return when one of their Lordships appeared to nod in approval of his submissions. This encouraged him to continue and finish his appeal.

However, my learned friend was shocked when he sat down to see the kindly Lord, who appeared to be agreeing with his submissions, stand up and say:
"Be upstanding for their Lordships."
Whereupon their Lordships stood up and filed out of the Chamber followed by their amiable clerk!

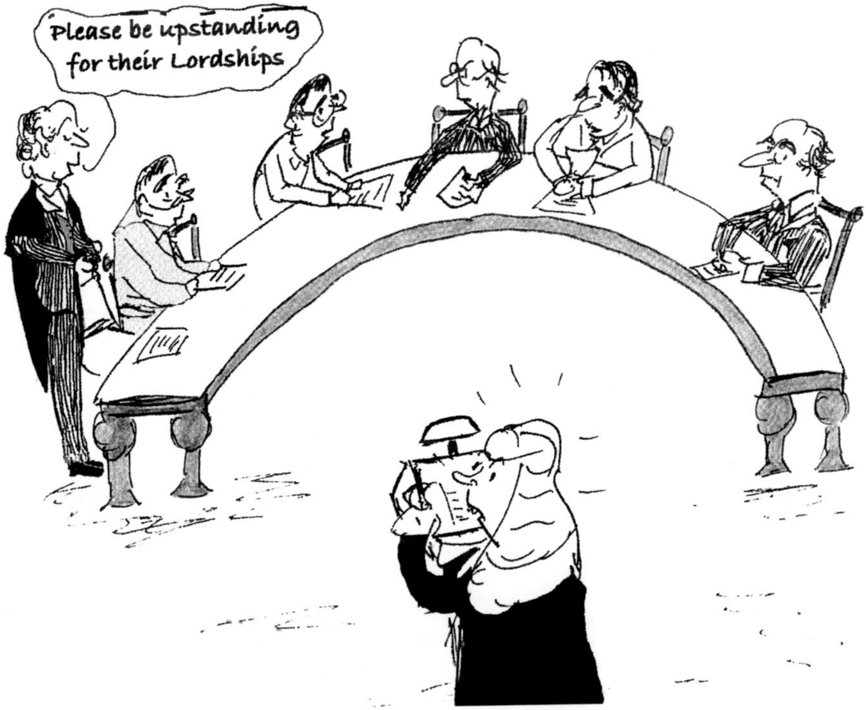
Please be upstanding for their Lordships

21. THE TURKS & CAICOS ISLANDS

A single judge in a British Dependency such as the Turks & Caicos Islands is at a great disadvantage in that he can no longer rely on the good nature of his colleagues on the Bench for advice or confirmation on matters of law or appropriate sentence of imprisonment. He is very much alone especially in a country where the indigenous population, by reason of their culture and upbringing, sometimes take a different view of certain cases.

I was very much aware of this problem at an early stage in my tenure as Chief Justice. So I decided to send copies of my sentence and sentencing remarks to the local radio station to be broadcast together with my reasons for passing such a sentence. I duly drafted out a communiqué for the media and handed it to my new secretary to type. An hour or so later my enthusiastic young secretary returned with the typed version and to my horror the text concluded:

'The sentence imposed will be accompanied by the Chief Justice's senseless remarks.'

She may have been right but I did not consider it a good policy to have it proclaimed to all the islanders!

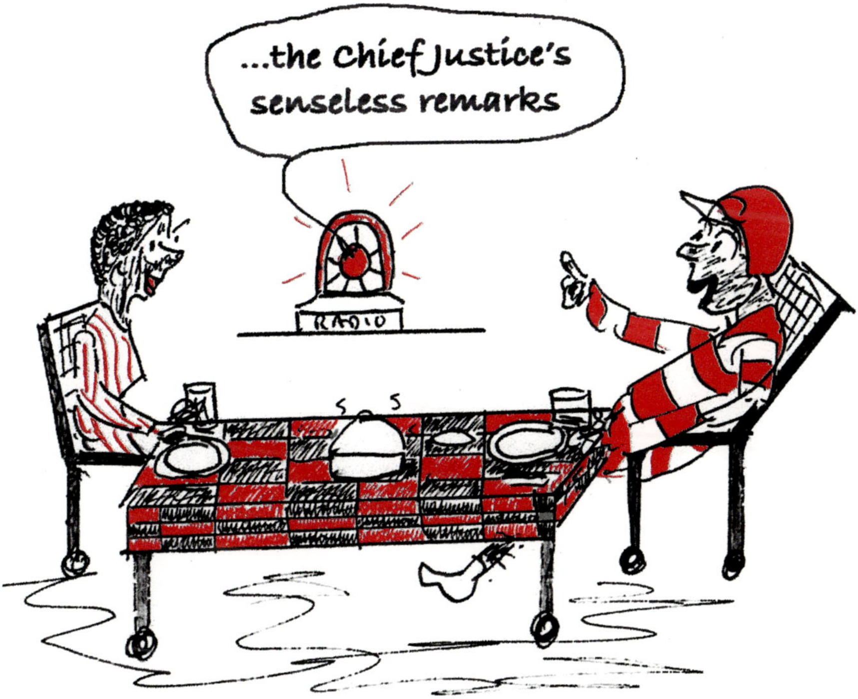
...the Chief Justice's
senseless remarks
RADIO

22. A SENIOR SOLICITOR'S DAY IN COURT

A senior partner in a well-known city firm of solicitors suddenly discovered to his horror that an important document, that should have been filed in the list of documents in a long complex commercial case now before the High Court, was not included. As time was on the wing he decided to go to court in person and apply for the document to be listed.

On the appointed day, he duly appeared in court attired in gown and band, but of course no wig. He sat patiently listening to the Bar and Bench deal with various matters succinctly, eruditely and sometimes with wit. He became slightly nervous due to his inexperience as an advocate but when his case was called on he rose to his feet and said:

"May it please your Lordships," (he got that right) "I would like to mention at the outset that I am a little hard of hearing."

"That's all right," chirped one of the judges, "we can hear you perfectly well!"

I am a little hard of hearing
That's alright we can hear you perfectly well

23. MISCELLANY

A.   The Legendary Rigby Swift J

B.   Overseas Judges

C.   A Victorian Poison-Murder Case

D.   A Barrister's Attempt to be Humorous

E.   Three Snippets:

        (i)   As God Be My Witness

        (ii)   A Judge's Plea

        (iii)   A Juror's Plea

A. THE LEGENDARY RIGBY SWIFT J.

Judges, yes, could be impatient but then counsel could also be long winded. A story told to me, which I cannot confirm, was about a legendary character; a judge by the name of Rigby Swift who was on the scene before I arrived and by all accounts he was a colourful High Court Judge, much respected and liked by those who had to appear in front of him.

On one occasion he was sitting in the Divisional Court in London, listening to a pompous QC making submissions that were interminable. Eventually, his patience was tried so he interrupted counsel and said:
"Mr X, there is no jury here."
The QC politely bowed, then continued and soon was being just as verbose as he was before.
The judge's patience was tried to the limit and eventually he decided to interrupt yet again.
He spoke to the court usher and said in more than a loud stage whisper:
"Usher, put the lights on in the jury box as Mr X doesn't believe me."

Usher, put the lights on in the Jury Box as Mr X doesn't believe me.

B. OVERSEAS JUDGES

I would like to pay tribute to Judges who did so much good work in establishing a respect for the rule of law in our Commonwealth. They had to cope with all sorts of problems that do not arise in this country.

The most successful Judges were those who were more sensitive to the communities they served, understanding the local and cultural beliefs and being prepared to bend the letter of the law to suit the circumstances of the case.

I will restrain myself to one example of how a judge had to deal with a situation which an English judge would not have had to face at home. One F B Simpson was sitting as a Magistrate in his court in Bengal when the court doors suddenly burst open and in rushed a distraught Indian carrying the mangled leg of his son. He cried out:
"What sort of ruler are you, sitting here arguing with lawyers when a tiger is eating my son?"

Simpson stared at the mangled leg for a few seconds, brought down his gavel and adjourned the court. He then went out and shot the tiger. Not a good example of the separation of powers (Judicial, Executive and Legislative) but he was a hero in the local community!

What sort of Ruler are you sitting here, arguing with lawyers when a tiger is eating my son?

C. A VICTORIAN POISON MURDER CASE

The national newspapers gave wide coverage to this notorious poison murder case. Briefly stated, the accused was alleged to have poisoned his wife with a concoction including the poison strychnine.

The defence counsel was putting up a sterling performance on behalf of his client until he came to cross examine the shopkeeper of the local hardware store who had testified that the accused had bought some strychnine from his shop some weeks before his wife's death.

In cross-examination of the shopkeeper the questions and answers were as follows:
Counsel: "The weather was hot at the time, was it not?"
Witness: "Yes sir."
Counsel: "There were many flies about at that time of year?"
Witness: "Yes sir, plenty."
Counsel: "You had, did you not, a number of customers buying fly paper at this time?"
Witness: "Oh, yes sir, many."
Counsel: "Well, how can you be sure that the accused was one of those many customers that bought flypaper from you?"
Witness: "Because he was the only one who asked if it contained strychnine, sir.

Because he was the only one who asked if it contained strychnine, Sir

D. A BARRISTER'S ATTEMPT TO BE HUMOROUS

I have avoided naming judges and barristers as far as possible but I am sure the late Fred Parsons would not take offence at being mentioned. He was a stocky little chap who ended up specialising in divorce cases. He was, it must be said, a showman who attempted to stand out as rather special. He would appear extremely confident and try to hold the centre stage with his eloquence that was often exaggerated and verbose.

On this occasion he opened a divorce case involving <u>Polish</u> nationals by saying:
"May it please your Lordship, this couple are <u>poles</u> apart."

Before he could say anything further the judge quickly interrupted him saying:
"Let's get on with, it shall we?"

Poor Fred, he should have known better!

In this case My Lord, the parties are poles apart...
Let's get on with it shall we?

Snippet 1: "As God be my witness..."

Snippet 2: Judge's Plea

Hanley County Court - an undefended divorce day. When respondents were failing to turn up and the Judge became frustrated!

Snippet 3: A Juror's Plea

The Author

David's sketches are world famous amongst his friends; they appear on Christmas cards, letters, and postcards. He was foremost a Circuiteer on the Oxford, now Midland Circuit. He liked the cut and thrust of the criminal trial as for him that is what advocacy is all about, persuading a Jury to see it your way. Later he went on the Bench, both here and overseas, but in his opinion, the law is never a bore.